LEARNING ABOUT SAGE AND SMUDGING

Learning About Sage and Smudging.

Series "Using Sage and Smudging"
By: Sherry Lee
Version 1.1 ~July 2022
Published by Sherry Lee at KDP
Copyright ©2022 by Sherry Lee. All rights reserved.

TABLE OF CONTENTS.

INTRODUCTION.

Different methods exist for aura and space purification. Using specific herbs to clear the region is a simple and easy method. It works! In this manner, herbs and incense have been utilized for thousands of years with good cause.

White Sage, a wonderfully aromatic herb that grows wild in the mountains of California, is one of the best all-purpose cleaners. Due to the herb's mystical attributes and the spirit that hovers over it, indigenous people have revered White Sage.

As soon as you inhale the aroma of White Sage being burned and used to smudge a space or aura, you can experience a condition of altered consciousness. I adore the aroma, but it is quite potent. It may repulse certain people, but that can be rather revealing in and of itself.

My experience has shown me that heavy smokers dislike the aroma of sage. Could it be that the frequency of it attempts to disrupt the smoker's cigarette smoking habit, causing the first discomfort?

Perhaps sage could be used to assist in overcoming this addiction. This herb's vibrational frequency will swiftly dislodge and eliminate most bad energies.

Have you ever felt uncomfortable in a home or facility with significant emotional turmoil, a funeral, or a protracted sickness? A thorough smudge with sage would likely have a potent effect and greatly assist in shifting the "vibes" there.

If someone has been unsuccessfully trying to sell such a home, they should strongly consider employing the sage smudging technique to clear and elevate the energy there. Afterward, they may discover that the property has a better "vibe" that a prospective buyer may also perceive. I wouldn't be shocked if it increased their prospects of receiving a buy offer shortly after that.

When higher frequency energy collides with lower frequency energy, the lower frequency energy is dislodged, shattered, expelled, and cleaned.

This GUIDE explores the elegant art of smudging with sage for purification and cleansing the home, workplace, etc.

Let's get started.

CHAPTER 1
WHAT IS SMUDGING, AND HOW DO I PERFORM IT?

Many modern belief systems contain smudging, which is widely employed in ceremonies and meditation. A smudging ceremony is spiritually and psychologically purifying since it eliminates negative energy.

Its history, the different ways it has been utilized over the past, and the complexities of its practice might fill a whole chapter. In a nutshell, smudging is based on ancient shamanic practices.

It is used to cleanse, purify, protect, establish peace and harmony and expel negative energy through the smoke produced by burning various plants. White Sage is one of the most popular and widely utilized herbs.

Smudging can be performed by using a smudge stick (a bundle of herbs, such as white sage, knotted into a stick shape for ease of handling) or by burning loose leaves in a fire-resistant container, such as a shell or a ceramic dish. It is a good idea to put sand or dirt on the bottom of a dish or shell to insulate it from the heat, making it more comfortable and safe to use.

Regular smudging can be a practical technique to maintain a sense of equilibrium and tranquility. It is especially helpful if you have been around individuals who are ill, depressed, afraid, angry, or emotionally distraught if you are feeling blue or melancholy or have been under considerable stress.

Self-smudging is a simple task. If using a smudge stick, light its end on a candle flame or with a long lighter. Hold the stick over the flame until a lot of smoke is produced and the stick burns properly. This is safer than a match because it takes a bit to get a cigarette lit.

Use your hand or a feather to fan the smoke over your body. Gently or softly waft the smoke over your body. You can begin from the top of the body and work your way down or from bottom to top, whichever is most comfortable for you. Get the back of your body as thoroughly as possible and, if possible, the soles of your feet.

If you use a smudge bowl or shell with loose leaves, light it with a long barbecue lighter or stove lighter until it is well smoking. Then, pass it over your body to bathe in the smoke. After smudging, individuals typically feel calmer, lighter, and brighter.

Smudge burning can be performed daily to purify and cleanse the body, office, and house of negative energies. Also, you can cleanse your crystals and any other objects you possess. As with all these actions, the significance of your intention is equal to that of the ritual and the smudge's physical components.

Smudging with sage is a fun way to purify crystals. It is a straightforward and effective method that can be applied to different stones.

Sage smudging is the cleansing of crystals using a sage smudge stick or dried sage on an incense burner. Crystal cleansing is crucial because it eliminates the energetic debris that can accumulate in the crystals' vibrational healing fields. This debris and energetic imprints can be removed through cleansing, restoring the crystal's high vibrational state for healing assistance.

The only disadvantages of sage smudging are that most people do not want to burn incense or light a smudge stick to cleanse a single crystal. This task should be postponed until you have multiple crystals to cleanse simultaneously. This is ideal if you have just completed a chakra crystal healing session and have 16 stones to cleanse. This method can cleanse as many or as few crystals as desired.

Simply light one end of a sage smudge stick and wait until the smoke is fully perceptible. Pass the crystal at least four times back and forth through the smudge smoke, turning after each pass. Therefore, one must pass through the smoke and return through it. One pass-through is back and forth. Thus, eight motions are required to cleanse a crystal thoroughly. This takes a few seconds to complete.

The same method applies when using dried sage and an incense burner; however, be careful not to burn your hand or crystal if the sage gets too close to the burner. Ensure that there is sufficient smoke emanating from the burner.

CHAPTER 2
SAGE IS A SACRED PLANT FOR MANY OF THE WORLD'S PEOPLE.

Common Sage (Salvia officinalis) is a member of the mint family, and its essential oil is sourced from Spain, Croatia, and France. It is known by the name "herba sacra" among the ancient Romans.

Salvia for the sage plant is derived from the word "salvation." Sage contains up to 50 percent ketones and is therefore not recommended for consumption. Sage clary is superior for internal usage.

Spanish Sage (Salvia lavandulifolia) was formerly regarded as a panacea in Spain; it was believed to improve longevity and protect against many illnesses, including plague. Sage has been used to treat various conditions, including respiratory infections, menstrual and digestive symptoms. It was thought to improve the senses and memory.

American Indians have always utilized sage for aura cleansing through smudging and sweat lodges. In the 12th century, Hildegard of Bingen described sage as warm, dry, and effective against sick humor. Also, she utilized it for intestinal issues.

How Can Sage Benefit Our Health Currently?

Sage is anti-tumor, hormone-regulating, estrogen-like, antifungal, antiviral, a stimulant for the circulatory system, and stimulates the gallbladder. It is utilized for menstruation issues such as PMS, estrogen deficits, progesterone, testosterone, and liver issues. It stimulates the mind and helps against depression and mental tiredness.

Sage applied topically has extremely potent estrogenic effects and can be beneficial for hot flashes, water retention, gum infections, and wrinkle prevention. It fortifies the energy centers, regulating the sacral chakra where repressed and abused emotions are held. It is used to prevent the graying of hair.

Sage is used to cleanse and purify the spirit. It is a spirit of protection for individuals who do not fear spiritual powers or the power of unseen beings. The principal impact is strengthening and aiding digestion, and it possesses estrogen-like properties. Use sage to promote strength, courage, tenacity, grounding, and protection for emotional healing.

Sage can be applied neat (undiluted) to the body, inhaled directly, or diffused by combining essential oil with one part of the mixing oil. Lavender blends beautifully with rosemary, citrus, hyssop, cedarwood, cypress, lemon-orange, basil, myrtle, petitgrain, peppermint, thyme, yarrow, rosewood, citronella, and pine.

Due to its high ketone level, it should be avoided by epileptic patients whose seizures are not effectively controlled by medication. It is not recommended for oral administration due to its high thujone concentration.

Spanish Sage should be avoided at all costs during pregnancy. It should also not be administered to those with estrogen-dependent malignancies. Are you interested in learning more about the medicinal qualities of sage and other essential oils? Consider obtaining aromatherapy certification.

Aromatherapy and healing energy courses can help you comprehend how essential oils heal the body/mind/spirit.

CHAPTER 3
THE ELEGANT CRAFT OF SMUDGING.

Physical or emotional healing cannot occur unless the individual is cleansed of any of the following conditions:

1) Emotional states characterized by wrath, bitterness, envy, jealousy, and guilt

2) Negative thoughts regarding individuals, the past, or the future

3) Negative emotions like sadness, hatred, and desire

4) Evil or negative spirits

5) Attachments or bad energy transmitted by others

In most Aboriginal traditions, a sweat lodge, a tent, teepee, or cave filled with smoke and heat is used to treat these diseases. Ancient Roman structures known as purgatories served the same function.

These smoke and heat-filled locations were revered as hallowed regions where spirits or God might remove undesirable entities and energies from a person without interfering with others.

Many indigenous civilizations worldwide employ the burning of herbs, plants, and resins for the same reason. In some cultures, smoke is smeared upon the body to darken it. This is how the present process became known as smudging.

In smudging ceremonies, the following herbs, plants, grasses, and resins are typically employed. To purify your space, you can light these items yourself and carry a bundle of them in a counter-clockwise circuit around your home. I strongly advise washing the body outside, as sage may burn quite quickly and produce a lot of spinning smoke that easily sets off the fire alarm.

Sage is the most often used ingredient for cleansing. Sage is derived from Salvia, which means "to heal." There are further sage variations that belong to the Artemisia plant family.

This includes mugwort, which is used for purification and defense. White sage is employed for purification and protection. The combination and burning of pine and white sage branches are thought to attract prosperity.

Cedar and Juniper branches - These evergreen branches have historically been used to cleanse, purify and safeguard one's possessions. Occasionally, they are used to create brooms that "sweep" the smoke into the dwelling during a house blessing.

Sweetgrass - This musty-smelling grass is believed to repel negative influences and attract positive ones. It is often employed after a prayer or ritual to "hold" the power.

This aromatic plant resin is mostly employed in South American rituals. The contact of copal's powerfully perfumed smoke is believed to cleanse and purify any object or individual.

Frankincense and Myrrh - these "biblical" resins are utilized in ceremonies and rituals across Africa, the Middle East, and Europe. When burned together, they are believed to balance yin and yang or the masculine and feminine energy in a space or residence. Either is said to bring good fortune into the home.

Tobacco - Tobacco smoke is used to send prayers to God, where they will be heard and answered. Combining tobacco with sage, cedar, or sweet grass is believed to improve the magical effects of a smudge.

Occult, new age, and gift shops sell smudges and resins for commercial sale. I typically place the branches, plants, or resins in the bowl and use them to stain my hands and face.

While performing these actions, I pray for divine protection, purification, and blessings. When treating another individual or cleansing a room, I occasionally use a feather or a branch to direct the smoke in the proper direction.

Smudging is not all voodoo and witchcraft. Individuals typically feel better after meditation and create a space for the free flow of positive energy and prayers. The practice is also said to generate negative ions in the air, eliminating static and generating a positive environment.

CHAPTER 4
HOW TO MAKE A SMUDGE STICK - CLEARING YOUR SPACE.

Have you ever had someone enter your home or business and leave an unpleasant odor? When this occurs, it is time to smudge! Native Americans, Celtic, and other ancient societies utilized smudging to cleanse, purify, clear, and release energy. It is utilized in many ceremonies and rituals to establish the tone and prepare the participants on an emotional, spiritual and psychic level.

It is often employed before meditation, prayer, or sweat lodge when individuals are ill or unhappy or simply to release stale, stagnant energy and generate a new flow. Smudging can be performed on the environment, body, and personal belongings.

Sagebrush is the most popular herb for smudging in my region. White sage, cedar, pine, pinion, juniper, sweetgrass, mugwort, tobacco, lavender, and different resins and roots are also commonly used for smudging.

Commonly, a bundle or stick is utilized for smudging. A second method involves placing the herbs in a pot. In either case, the herbs are ignited to create an ember-emitting smoke stream. This smoke is circulated clockwise around the area, person or objects.

During smudging, one may venerate the four cardinal directions and elements, Mother Earth and Father Sky, Grandmother Moon and Grandfather Sun, or anything else that seems fitting. An invocation can be used for healing, clarity, or other purposes, and this is an excellent moment to express appreciation and seek guidance.

You can use any herbs listed or a mix of them. I've developed a preference for cedar and sage because sage helps dispel bad energy, and cedar evokes positive energy. Regardless of the composition, the smoke will effectively transmute negative energy.

Some claim that the greatest time to harvest smudge sticks is in the spring, but I feel that they can be prepared at any time of year with the right intentions. The initial action is to collect the plant's branchlets. Always request permission from the plant devas and leave a "thank you" gift of hair, cornmeal, tobacco, or something similar.

Next, you will need some natural twine, such as jute, hemp, or cotton. Cut approximately 2 yards of twine. Lay down your herb cuttings; the cedar and sage will form a little roll, making them easier to wrap. Use enough material for an eight- to ten-inch stick with a four- to five-inch diameter.

Make a slip knot by tying a loop on one end of the twine and threading the other end through it. Then, pick up the herb stack, place the loop around the base and tighten it to secure. Now, continue wrapping the rope around the stick while maintaining moderate tension (if the string is too tight, it may not burn nicely).

When you have reached the top, continue winding down until you have just enough twine to tie back on itself. I use a crochet hook to re-thread the short thread. You now possess a customized smudge stick. Allow it to dry thoroughly before using.

You should practice smudging your space once each week, or you can simply ignite your smudge stick and cleanse whenever you feel the energy needs a better flow.

CHAPTER 5
HOW TO SMUDGE YOUR HOME USING A WAND OR BUNDLE OF SAGE.

Smudging is a cleansing ritual performed by burning a bundle of dried herbs (traditionally Sage, Copal, White Sage, Lavender, Cedar Sweetgrass, or a combination of these) to purify the physical body, locales, and personal belongings.

The practice of smudging is an element of many Native American traditions. This bundle of burning herbs is called a smudge bundle, smudge stick, or wand.

The practice of smudging or cleansing a space dates back to the earliest days of humanity. Most traditional civilizations, from the Zulu to the Maori, from the Chinese to the Balinese, practice cleansing and blessing rites with ancient roots. Native American smudging extends back hundreds of years.

Even the incense billowing through a church or temple cleanses and purifies the place as certainly as a medicine man's bowl of sacred smoke/smudge.

It has been scientifically shown that smudging has a favorable effect on the environment's energy. The negative ions in the smoke and the smoke molecules capture the positive (unhealthy) ions, purifying the air. As a result, as the smoke clears (ideally out the window), it carries the negative energy (positive ions) with it, dissipating it outside.

The advantages of smudging your home are many. It will improve every area of your life since it releases all the negative energy. Energy adheres to walls and becomes stuck in corners, especially emotionally charged energy. You can be responding to energy from prior homeowners without even realizing it. If you continue to have the same debate in the same room in your home, it's time to paint!

This is a step-by-step lesson on how to smudge your home. This is how I smudge, although there are different other methods. As you smudge your space more often, you will undoubtedly develop your ritual rhythm, with variations in the phrases you say and the gestures you perform.

Essential Items: *Gallon Size Bag/s * *Incense *Matches Rubber Band/s *Smudge Bundle *Candle *Fireproof Ceramic Bowl or Shell for Ashes Collection

Gather your belongings in the middle of your home, preferably near the sink. Locate your smoke detectors and cover each with a plastic bag secured with a rubber band. This keeps the smoke detector from activating due to all the smudge smoke!

Create as many windows as you can.

The candle is lit using a match, which is subsequently doused with water to guarantee that it is extinguished.

Hold the end of the Smudge Bundle that is not wrapped over the flame. You wish for it to catch fire and smoke. Ensure that the center is ignited by blowing on it multiple times. Hold the Bowl or Shell beneath the bundle at all times to capture the ashes that occasionally fall off.

Smudging one's chakras and oneself.

Simply hold the smudge bundle and Bowl together in front of you, beginning at the feet and moving slowly up the body. Then, hold the smudge and Bowl/Shell at the base of your spine for a few seconds to ensure that the smoke travels up your back. Imagine a healing white light enveloping you while the smoke purges you of all bad and stale energy.

Proceed to the front door. Declare aloud, while you move your hands around the door's seams, "I cleanse this area and all inside it of any negative or stale energy." Start traveling along the house's wall to the right of the front door (or clockwise).

Repeat the preceding phrase as you proceed. It isn't necessary to "cover" the entire wall with smoke; simply go gently along it. As you approach windows or doors, be sure to "close" the entire frame with smoke and linger for a few seconds longer in corners, where stagnant surplus energy tends to collect.

Continue around the house's perimeter until you return to the front door. Seal it with smoke once more. All the previous bad, lingering or stagnant energy in your home has been neutralized. Now, the area must be infused with new, healthy, pleasant energy.

Using your candle, ignite the incense and allow the flame to burn down to a smolder, ensuring it does not go out. Declare that 'the smoke from this incense infuses this house and all its contents with bright, healthy, new positive energy.' now, you can go around the house again with your incense or utilize ash catchers to place incense in the corners of your home to burn through.

Ensure that all the incense sticks are extinguished before discarding them by immersing them in water. Place the end of the smudge bundle under running water to extinguish it. It will heat up before extinguishing your candle; express gratitude to the Universe for assisting you in purifying your home. Then extinguish it.

Remove the bags from your smoke detectors at this time. Keep the windows open until the smoke has passed. If the odor is so strong, you can place air fresheners throughout the home.

You have done it! Take some moment to get a feel for your home. Doesn't it feel considerably lighter? Establish a routine of smudging your home regularly. Remember that intense emotions leave an energy imprint that affects everyone interacting with it. Regular smudging eliminates these heated places. When working with fire, please remember to adopt common-sense safety precautions.

CHAPTER 6
UTILIZING SMUDGING TO REMOVE NEGATIVE ENERGIES AND INFLUENCES FROM YOUR RESIDENCE.

Smoking or smudging is a Native American method of purification. White sage is typically used, although other herbs, such as sweet grass and cedar, are often employed. Many commercial smudge sticks are comprised of sage and cedar bundled together.

Once burned, the smoke from the smudge wand (or sage pieces if using a smudge pot) is used to coat the body or artifacts (scared objects: pipes, feathers, flutes, dancing regalia, etc.) that require cleansing and purification.

Collecting smoke with cupped hands and rubbing it over the "ethnic" body (the aura) is customary. In addition, feather fans are utilized to help distribute the smoke across the entire person or item. Smudge pots can be made from different materials, including clay pots, iron holders, or the most frequent abalone shells.

The practice of smudging is seen as a kind of prayer and a powerful connection to the Spirit, thus equating to a blessing and a shield. It is also common to smudge a home or vehicle.

When unpleasant events have occurred, or undesirable negative entities are present in the home. It is a good approach to "wipe the slate clean" and provide a sensation of cleanliness. It assists in dissipating the energy and enables us to begin anew.

While smudging, you might recite a prayer to be used for communicating with Spirit. Tina Michelle wrote this Native American Prayer.

Grandfather

When I contemplate the Great Spirit,

the Most Holy One

I consider the tender affection of a grandfather.

Therefore, I beg you, Grandfather:

to listen to my prayers

Grandfather, bless my feet so that they may walk a decent road.

Bless my knees so that I may pray with humility.

Bless my stomach so that I may never experience hunger.

Bless my heart so that I may always act lovingly.

Bless my arms so that I may bear my dear ones' troubles.

Bless my hands so that they only produce wonderful things.

Bless my shoulders so they can bear the weight of my actions.

Bless my throat so that I might speak kindly.

Bless my eyes with the ability to look past the horizon.

Bless my thoughts so that I may be receptive and merciful.

Thank you, grandfather, for all these benefits.

It's great!

"According to what we have been taught, some plants have entered into a sacred agreement with us two-leggeds: in exchange for our respectful treatment of them, they will give up their lives so that we may use their purifying smoke to cleanse and pray, so that we may maintain our equilibrium and walk in a sacred manner. This implies that we are to harvest the plants respectfully, requesting permission and expressing gratitude, taking only what we need without harming the plant.

"You can use the following smudging ritual as a template or devise your own. There is no right or wrong way. Place the abalone shell right in front of you and, vocally or in silence, thank it for the life that created it and for assisting you in this ritual.

Place the herb(s) you will be using in the shell and express gratitude as you do so. They died so that you could smoke this cigarette. This should not elicit guilt but rather appreciation for the sacrifice. One day, you will donate your body to other Earthlings.

Next, ignite the smoke mixture. As you release the flame, thank Father Sun, the source of all fires, and the spirit of Fire for assisting you with this rite. Ensure that a portion of each plant you have placed in the bowl is ignited.

Thus, the smoke will include all the energies you've chosen to employ. With your feather, gently fan the fire until the herbs are burning sufficiently to produce sufficient smoke. Use the feather to extinguish the fire with one or two swift strokes. If the soot appears to be dying, fan it hard until it resumes smoking. If the flame goes out, it is OK to reignite it.

Using both hands as a cup, inhale the smoke directly into your heart. Catch additional smoke and pass it down your neck after passing it over your head. Pass the smoke with each hand, one at a time, along the opposing arm and hand.

Then, using both hands, inhale further smoke into your abdomen and exhale it via your legs to the earth. This procedure purifies our emotions, brains, and bodies and grounds us. It is comforting to see the smoke remove any worries or bodily ailments while performing this task.

You can now smear objects by passing them through the smoke from the four cardinal directions, beginning with the East. Request that the object is purified for your use or distribution. If you are smudging with other individuals, smudge yourself first and hold the shell by its edges for the other individuals to smudge.

Also, you can smudge a house or room that requires cleansing. Pass the smoldering smudge around the room and use your feather to force any negative energy out through an open door or window. Allow the ashes to cool before returning them to the earth with care. Respect this ceremony and carefully dispose of the ashes, thanking the herbs and the fire once more.

Many individuals smudge before any other ceremony, at the beginning of the day, or before and after an important debate. This is a serious event for us.

After performing it, we feel better, have more energy, and have a better day, and it is beneficial to cleanse your home to eliminate any stagnant energy periodically. Understand that the sacred intent of two-leggeds is what opens the door for these spirits to work with us during ceremonies.

Sage's power is the ability to repel negative forces. Sage from California (with broad leaves) and sage from the desert (with smaller leaves) can be used interchangeably or even simultaneously, but most people prefer one over the other.

The ability of sweet grass to attract beneficial energy.

Its pleasant aroma makes ourselves and our objects more pleasant in spirit. Before it is collected, it is sometimes referred to as the hair of the Earth Mother and is braided with affection in the field.

The evergreens, including cedar, juniper, and pinion pine, create equilibrium and harmony.

Lavender offers a soothing effect.

Rose petals evoke the strength of the heart.

STEPS REQUIRED TO PERFORM A SMUDGING RITE.

Sage, sweet grass, cedar, or tobacco, alone or in combination or other plants; a shell or a bowl fashioned from natural materials (clay, pottery); a feather or fan; matches; sand or fine soil are required.

1. Combine the plants to be used and place them in a shell or strong bowl, then light them. Some herbal mixes do not burn well. You can need to start by placing a charcoal briquette in the basin. Make sure there is dirt or sand in the bottom of the bowl or shell before burning the charcoal or the plants. This will ensure that it is not too hot to hold.

2. Use a fan or a feather from a domesticated bird (chicken, turkey, pheasant, or duck) to extinguish the flame after lighting the plants. Throughout the ritual, you must fan the plants to keep them ablaze.

- Eagle feathers are not permitted in possession of non-Indians.

3. Once the herbs are smoking, inhale the smoke (just the smoke, not the bowl) to the heart, then over the head, down the arms, and the front of the body.

Now, direct the smoke over your back and toward the ground. If you need extra balancing or healing in a certain area of your body, you can accentuate the area by drawing smoke to it.

You are responsible for cleansing your energy field. The plants assist. They do not act for you.

Next, present smoke to the six directions in the following order: up to the Creator, down to the Earth, then to the north, east, south, and west.

After smudging yourself and offering the smudge, you can hold the bowl while others smear themselves or smudge them personally. They should inhale the smoke first to the heart, then over the head, down the arms, the chest, and the back.

You can now go around the area you intend to use while wafting the smoke. If you are indoors, smudge the room's walls, giving special attention to the corners.

Smoke any medicinal tools that will be used during rituals.

You can personalize this Smudging Ceremony to meet your cleansing requirements at the moment. Make the necessary adjustments for us to perform a space clearing and cleansing to rid your house and family of disruptive bad spirits.

CHAPTER 7
SMUDGING TO REMOVE NEGATIVE ENERGY FROM YOUR HOME OR OFFICE.

We are all always on the move, whether for work, school, socializing, having guests over, shopping, or even talking on the phone, to mention a few activities. We are in continual contact with other individuals, settings, and spaces in all aspects of our daily lives.

People leave behind both positive and bad energy wherever they go, but the negative energies have the greatest impact on us. A person may have a poor day and feel negative; they may be angry, have gotten into a fight, feel ill, etc. Over time, these bad energies will collect in your house, workplace, and within yourself, causing you to feel out of balance and stuck.

Everyone is influenced by negative energies, even though some of us, particularly youngsters, are more sensitive to them than others. You can feel drained, exhausted, and lacking in energy or hyperactive, restless, and irritable, which is quite common in children.

You can also be unable to settle or have trouble sleeping, not feel like your usual self, and feel uneasy. Still, you cannot pinpoint the cause, lack motivation, be emotionally scattered, and are generally on edge. Everyone reacts differently to these negative energies, whether light, moderate or severe.

Therefore, it is crucial to purify oneself and one's environment at home and work to avoid being impacted by these energies and maintain calm and equilibrium.

A simple and effective method of cleansing is the practice of White Sage Smudging.

It is well recognized to raise the vibration of any room, person, or object, cleansing, purifying, and removing all types of negativity. Smudge sticks can be used to cleanse, purify and protect the aura of a person, home, or business.

Traditionally, smudging feathers are used to delicately sweep and direct the smoke (like the Native Americans of North America do) but using your hand is also acceptable.

- Using a white sage smudge stick, ignite it over a fire-resistant container until it begins to burn, then extinguish the flame, and the smudge stick will smoke.

- Using your hand or a smudging feather, sweep the sage smoke over your head and down the front and back of your body, then repeat on the other side. You transfer the smoke through your aura (the energetic field surrounding your entire body).

- You can also do this with your children and other family members.

Depending on what you and your family have been doing, this can be performed daily, twice, or thrice each week or weekly.

Follow your gut and the emotions and behaviors of you and your family.

A simple and effective method for environmental sanitation:

- Begin with sage smudging by lighting the sage in the same manner as personal cleansing and closing all windows and doors.

- Walk through your home, workplace, or place of business while sweeping the smoke from each room. Take great care to smudge the room's corners, as negative energy may readily migrate to corners, cupboards, and cabinets, creating a highly sluggish vibe in the area. Other than the space itself, be directed to the location where you believe negative and sluggish energy exists.

- Once the house or location has been thoroughly smudged, Frankincense granule incense is burned.

- Place a charcoal tablet in a bowl or incense container filled with rock salt or sand designed for this purpose. Using tongs, hold the charcoal tablet over the bowl and light it from underneath while holding it over the bowl. Place the charcoal back in the bowl once it has caught fire (you'll know when sparks appear).

Place a few frankincense granules on the charcoal. Once smoking is permitted, allow the smoke to permeate each room. You can have multiple bowls of frankincense burning at once, particularly if you are clearing your home, as each room must be purified.

Allow it to burn in each room for around 5 to 10 minutes. Open all doors and windows upon completion of each room to allow the negative energy to escape.

For a full cleansing, doing both sage smudging and frankincense is essential. The sage will dislodge and raise negative energy, but the frankincense ensures these energies are released and depart the being cleansed home or region. This can be done every two weeks or every month, depending on your circumstances.

The energy of a location is affected by illness, violence, disagreements, drug usage, thoughts, and emotions. When you enter a person's house or business, a portion of your mind automatically registers the atmosphere. Whether conscious or not, this awareness is a survival mechanism that keeps you vigilant for protection and safety.

I occasionally visit "open houses" in our community to satiate my curiosity about what kind of homes are selling for what prices. These dwellings all reveal information about their occupants.

In some households, the energy is so intense that it is difficult to breathe. If real estate agents were aware of how this energy impacts the subconscious of prospective purchasers, they would remove the home's energy before listing it for sale.

Clearing a location resets its energy. It is essential to cleanse the energy, like cleaning dirty flooring in a new home. This energy may not be visible, but that does not mean it does not exist. Before bringing anything inside your new home or office, you should clear the area. Otherwise, you are living in the energetic filth of another person, which can damage you.

Near Boston, I once explored a famous old home. Our little group was told about the original residents of the house, who resided there when the "shot heard 'around the world" was fired. When we entered a bedroom on the second floor, I not only felt but also smelled illness. It was one of those places where I had difficulty breathing, a sign that the energy was stagnant.

I stated, "Someone with a protracted sickness probably passed away in this room." The tour guide and others regarded me as though I had sprouted a second head. The guide then confirmed the death of an older woman. I knew she was still present in some capacity.

People's energy does not leave with them when they leave. It adheres to walls, curtains, upholstery, carpet, and the air. When I relocated, I inquired about the status of the previous occupants. How was their connection, budget, and temper?

This is consistent with the ancient concept of Feng Shui, which instructs us to learn the home's history and previous occupants before moving in. For instance, if someone were unwell or fell on hard times financially or otherwise, it would be unwise to move in behind them because the same fate could befall you.

This can also be advantageous. The downstairs tenants of a two-story duplex where I once resided began as single women and left as newlyweds.

We will not always know the history of a property before moving in. As a general rule, I would therefore clear any house or building. Every room should be meticulously cleaned, the walls wiped down, the carpets and floors shampooed and fresh air circulated.

Bring in much light from outside. In addition to sounds, chanting, singing, living plants, fresh flowers, and certain possible crystals, energy can be moved and transformed with the aid of sonic, vocal, vegetative, floral, and crystal elements.

Use further cleaning techniques when something feels odd, or you know there was negativity or death. The one I use most often comes from Native American tradition. A Native American medicine man explained this technique to me years ago in the hills around Lake Arrowhead.

A buddy had recently purchased a neighboring fixer-upper with such a terrible vibe that we refused to enter any rooms. We asked the medicine man to come to our home, but he indicated that it wasn't a good day for him and that we should handle it ourselves.

He recommended using a bundle of white sage, a Native American herb, wrapped tightly (sometimes called a smudge stick or sage wand). If it is windy, open all the windows or crack them slightly. Open cabinets and closet doors.

Match the sage tips and extinguish the flame, causing the wand to smoke faintly. Circulate in a circular direction around the house and enter each room. Allow each nook, cabinet, and closet to be filled with smoke. Pass past again in a clockwise direction when finished.

Sage alone leaves a void, so combining it with another herb, such as lavender or sweet grass, is recommended. This attracts more positive energy as the negative energy leaves.

Use your purpose to bring in higher, more positive energy if you only have sage. Our medicine man also suggested that we sprinkle sea salt in the corners of the house and leave white candles lit (with supervision).

There are different methods for clearing a place. I've discovered that a thorough cleaning and simple application of sage is typically sufficient. Sage can be used continuously to reset the energy of a space following any disturbance.

Spring is an excellent time to "smudge" your home or place of business. At any time of the year, "smudging" or "cleaning the space of any negative energies" can be performed. However, the Spring provides a certain type of "forward energy" that can strengthen any goal or attempt.

According to Eastern medicine, the energy of Spring is "anger, pressing through and occasionally violent." This energy is essential for new life to emerge from the ground, displacing the earth and making room for new life to thrive. Perhaps you have observed in your own life that spring is a season of rebirth and rejuvenation. Perhaps even new opportunities arise often for you throughout this season.

When you smudge your home or office at this time, you generate additional opportunities in your life today and set a purpose for the upcoming months. Start by cleaning your home. If you want to optimize the positive effects of smudging, you should also purge your closets and drawers of items you haven't worn or used in the past year.

Some individuals want to sell their old clothes/stuff, which is good and beneficial, but if you can afford it, I encourage you to donate the items instead (it's also a tax deduction!). This action increases your good energy because it awakens a spirit of generosity and a sense of abundance within you.

What can you use to smear your home? Holy Wood is my preferred fragrance because it "brings the forest indoors." Some prefer Sage, while others prefer rosewater; however, it is irrelevant. The aim is far more significant than the aroma. The ideal indicator is something to which you have an immediate positive reaction.

Stand at your front door and say, "I cleanse this area of all negative energy, sending them back into the light from where they came. This room now invites love, joy, money, abundance, and good health." While speaking these words, ignite your smudge stick and walk around the room's perimeter. The objective is to remove all negative energy from the room and fill the voids with love and joy.

I "see" pictures that are locked or impeding positive energies when I "clean" homes and workplaces. If this occurs, simply send these ideas and images into the light to be purified. As you smear the rooms, you can see "solutions" to trouble spots in your home.

Concern yourself less with the specific words you use and more with the concept of cleansing each room and establishing the intention for what you want the room (and your life) to attract.

After smudging all sections of your home, you can also smudge the yard if you so choose. Otherwise, return to your home. Play some wonderful music. Have something tasty to eat and drink as you daydream. Imagine the life you wish to live in your home. Consider the love, hope, and opportunities waiting for you to step into them and, most importantly, have fun!

CHAPTER 8
THE PROCESS OF CLEANING YOUR MINERALS AND GEMSTONES.

If you use stones and minerals in your visualization and inner work, it is crucial to purge them of bad energy and replenish them with positive ones. Periodically clearing your stones dispels negativity accumulated due to a stone's history or previous work for you.

It also recharges your tool, like a dead battery, and refreshes its power, much like a good night's sleep does for your body. (In a sense, it is only polite to clear and restore a mineral ally. as you would any item you've used and certainly want a friend to be treated!)

A clearing ritual resets and renews the stone's energy so that it can reconnect with its powers and purpose. The ritual itself refocuses your intent to use the stone and its assets, reaffirms your connection to it, and synchronizes the vibration of your respect and purpose with that of the stone you are employing.

Probably the most essential aspect of this ceremony is your desire. You have various possibilities, ways, and recommendations considered conventional in gemstone work. Still, since your mind, spirit, and goals are the most significant aspects of your spiritual life and work, you must do what seems appropriate and comfortable.

There are no inflexible criteria. If one way of clearing stones is effective, you should employ it. If you enjoy different combinations, feel free to include them all. Change the order of the exercises if anything feels pleasant or appropriate at one moment but not at another. Trust your intuition above all else. If you feel compelled to create your rituals, that is also completely OK.

Utilize sage smoke to cleanse and purify the energies of your stones. Sage smudges are a common method for removing negative energies from objects, spaces, rooms, buildings, etc., and can be bought in many metaphysical and health food stores.

Brush the stone in a counter-clockwise circle with your hands or roll it counter-clockwise in your palms as you announce that the stone's beneficial energies are being strengthened and realigned. After finishing this practice, softly blow on the stone to ensure that the harmful energy has been dispersed and removed from the stone's aura.

Water is a fantastic cleaning, of course. Use rainwater, snowmelt, or water from a natural lake or stream whenever possible. Even while using fresh water to wash and cleanse their stones, some individuals like to add sea salt to the water. Yes, you can use tap water, but you should let it sit for a few days to allow some of its pollutants and additives to evaporate.

Some individuals prefer to use water set out under either the New Moon or the Full Moon to obtain a certain charge. Water energized during the New Moon is very effective for launching initiatives or energies related to the zodiac sign where the New Moon is located.

Water energized during the Full Moon is useful for working with relationships, making decisions, and manifesting things. Again, the Full Moon polarity energies must be considered when using this procedure.

You can slowly warm a stone over the flame of a candle (NOT in the flame itself but just enough to warm the stone itself.) or place it on a hearth to be warmed by the fire.

As a means of anchoring its energies or returning it "home" to the environment where it has existed for thousands of years before being your ally and where it will likely return when you are gone, you might rebury the stone in the dirt for a time.

A stone used in intense or traumatic healing may require special care to recharge its energies, just as you would enable a live organism to recuperate and rest after exerting itself. You might freeze or place the stone in the snow in extreme circumstances. Limit its molecular action, just as you would allow a sick or exhausted person or animal to sleep to recover.

When you believe it has regained its willingness to serve you, gradually recharge it using one or more of the abovementioned methods. It may take multiple attempts before you believe your stone has regained its full strength and utility. Consider your gut before making this selection.

CHAPTER 9
HOW TO SMUDGE A CRYSTAL BALL WITH SAGE.

Diverse cultures have utilized crystal balls as sacred implements for thousands of years. It is essential to remember that crystals are sacred tools and to store them on your altar or in another sacred location when they are not in use. It is also recommended to cover your crystal ball with a black cloth while it is not in use to prevent light from reaching it.

I like to sleep with a fresh crystal ball or other sacred stone for at least four nights to begin creating a connection. During this period, your crystal ball will likely reveal its identity to you (after being cleansed).

When addressing your crystal ball, be careful to use its proper name. There will be a personal connection with your crystal ball. Thus, you should not allow others to handle or touch it.

You should also supply a specific bag or box to transport your crystal ball. Use this bag or box exclusively for your crystal ball.

As with any other sacred object, your crystal ball must be cleansed often. Before and after every use, I smudge my crystal ball with sage or sweetgrass. You can discover many other recommended cleansing procedures with a little investigation.

Using Your Magic Eight Ball.

Purify the crystal ball. Using your favorite method, you should always cleanse your crystal before each use.

Turn off all artificial lights, draw the curtains and darken the room. A lit candle should be a background light source in an otherwise dark room.

Use a white candle representing purity or a purple candle representing a higher spiritual aim.

As you proceed, you can utilize different colors based on your objectives for the session. Indicate that you will only permit positive energies to enter, or the door will be open to any energy. I like to construct a circle to work in by purifying and guarding the area with sage smoke.

Relax and take long, rhythmic breaths. Permit all stress and negativity to leave your body with each exhalation. Ground yourself and, as you inhale, draw in the energy of the Light; then, center your thoughts on the session's objective and respectfully request that the answers be revealed.

When you are relaxed, centered, and focused, open your eyes and allow them to drift to a location on the crystal ball to which you feel drawn. Allow your eyesight to become hazy (as if daydreaming) and fixate your eyes on the target while allowing your daydreaming gaze to travel through and past the target. Simply allow this to occur; do not attempt to compel it.

Clear your mind of all ideas and maintain deep, rhythmic breathing to achieve a state of light meditation. At this point, your crystal may become smoky, clouded, or darker. Allow this to occur without interrupting your meditation. If you lose your meditative state, simply restart your practice.

Remember that practice makes perfect! You can start to see visuals, feel emotions and hear communications. Don't attempt to explain, analyze or make sense of your experience at this moment; just go with the flow. Simply unwind and allow it to occur.

Also, ensure that you aren't attempting to generate photos as you would like to see them. Set aside personal judgments, wishes and desires, halt your thoughts and ideas, and be receptive to what the crystal ball reveals, even if it is not what you desire or believe it should be.

The stone will raise or reduce your vibration and bring you into the balance and harmony required for spiritual connection, allowing for effortless conversation. In addition, you can experience physical sensations like tingling, vibration, heat, or cold. This is typical.

Notate what you observe in your crystal ball. Initially, you can have trouble recalling what you observe during the session. Have a pencil and notepad on hand and try to record everything you observe.

Maintain your meditative state and concentration while writing or speaking into the recorder. This will require practice, as speaking or writing will begin to break you out of your trance state. A tape recorder can also record visual data.

By practicing walking meditation, you can strengthen your capacity to maintain a meditative state during physical exercise. Utilize the same approach of deep, rhythmic breathing, tension release, relaxation, blurred vision, and cleansing your mind of thoughts. I enjoy practicing walking meditation in the woods when going along a nature trail.

After your session, allow yourself to return to the physical presence. Refocus your eyes, take deep breaths and re-establish your physical grounding. Be conscious of your emotions at this time.

As you sever the connection with your crystal, you can feel your energy shift. You can feel refreshed as if you just awoke from a nap and feel energized. For complete grounding, consume a little snack and some water.

Return your crystal ball to its appointed spot on your altar or sacred space after cleansing it. Thank your crystal ball for its assistance.

Learning to use your crystal ball efficiently will require some practice. Be patient. Do not become disheartened if the first few attempts fail. Be determined, and it will function when you finally connect with your crystal ball.

CHAPTER 10
SMUDGING TECHNIQUE
FOR AN ENERGETIC
CLEARING OF AN AREA.

In this chapter, we'll discuss removing negative energies from a space-house, office, warehouse, or other location. There are many conventional methods for removing the energy debris left by trauma and negative ideas.

Suppose you've ever stepped into a haunted area and experienced the heebie-jeebies. In that case, you know what I'm referring to that strange, anxiety-inducing sensation that makes you want to flee as quickly as possible.

Even our homes and workplaces can have a negative aura, and a traumatic event is not required for this to occur. When people experience fear and amplify it by giving their emotions free reign, it imprints on the space's ethers.

After that, the negative energy might attract additional negative energies to the area, amplifying the effect. The bad environment then attracts disembodied souls who have spent a lifetime in such energies and feel very at home there. The entities might then attach themselves to the individuals who utilize the places.

Where do you most often encounter individuals that follow you and drain your vitality? Examples are hospitals, bars, cemeteries, slaughterhouses, conflict zones, etc. Wherever there is accumulated fear, there are typically many not-so-dangerous things waiting for a ride to a safer location. Ask skilled ghost hunters; they will describe their rituals to avoid picking up ghostly hitchhikers.

One can either cleanse the room independently or assist skilled individuals depending on one's religious or spiritual views. Removing the previous residents' negative energy, both living and dead, and any other negative energies are advisable when moving into a new area.

This is traditionally accomplished by prayer, smudging, drum or horn, crystals, music, salt, and chanting. Please choose your favorite and use it while moving in or out and at the end or beginning of the year.

To keep the space's energies clean, it is also helpful to undertake periodical clearing ceremonies. Even less energy sensitivity can feel the change in a cleared area. In my prior workplace, located at the rear of a small courtyard complex, I was often interrupted by individuals asking to use my restroom.

As a result of the unpleasant odors they left behind in my small office space, I felt compelled to ask the next applicant why he had bypassed every other office on his way back to mine. He pondered, "I don't know. It simply felt secure here."

An aromatic plant, such as sage, cedar, sandalwood, amber, or pine, is used for smudging.

You can either light a bundle of the leaves or resin on fire and blow it out, fanning the smoke into corners, closets, and cupboards, or you can ignite a bundle of the leaves or resin on fire and blow it out (being careful not to spread any sparks).

If you prefer not to utilize fire, you can use a few drops of the plant's essential oil in a spray bottle containing water. Use common caution while using either so you don't set something on fire or damage your best curtains with oily water drops.

Noises like a drum, horn, or handclaps can help rid a place of negative energy. Certain music frequencies and metal or crystal bowl clear energy (Tibetan brass bowls or crystal sounding bowls).

For cleansing people, frog choruses with rain are extraordinarily effective (warn the person to stay close to the toilet since they will likely be purging from every orifice-especially if combined with Reiki).

In command form, we send our Intent out into the ethers and summon in the higher power energies of enlightened/ascended masters such as Jesus, Buddha, the Great Mystery, Ra, etc., when we pray and sing. Generally, prayers and chants are performed in one of the other ways (incense for Buddhists, Hindus, and Christians, sage for Native Americans).

Charged salt is protective and is utilized in extreme circumstances. Salt may be dispersed as granules, mixed in water, placed in glasses about the room, blended with alcohol, and burned. Salt can also be added to bathwater to purify the aura. Salt has a long history of being carried in a wallet for financial security.

Start at the front door and proceed clockwise through each room, opening every door, drawer, and cabinet as you go. Bring assistance and make sure the doors and windows are slightly ajar when performing a cleansing to expel undesirable things (it is more common than you might think to have a window broken as the nasty makes haste to exit).

For severely clogged places, I propose walking in a circle around the entire structure after cleaning the area. Go three times counterclockwise and four or more times clockwise, always in that order, mindfully (don't let anyone bother you, don't answer if they try to talk to you, and don't stop at any point).

This concentrates all the negative energy at the center, where they are then dispersed by the counterclockwise rounds, much like the sun melting ice into steam. Ensure that the clockwise circles always outnumber the counterclockwise circles by at least one.

A neighbor's experience demonstrates that this final ritual is effective immediately. A young couple with two small sons moved into the apartment next to me, which had previously been inhabited by a very unpleasant Satanist and his drama-queen mother.

On the mother's side, the walls were lined with shelves filled with dolls; on the son's side, who knows what? The entire time they resided in that flat, there was nonstop screaming of obscenities, and the skinny, pimple-faced jerk never missed a chance to insult me anytime he saw me.

Approximately two weeks after the young couple moved in, they realized something was amiss. The lads who slept in the satanist's chamber began experiencing nightmares, fighting, and behaving terribly towards their parents.

The young mother was unaware of what had occurred. As we exchanged hello one day, she remarked that she believed moving there had been a mistake, given that their lives had taken a sharp downward turn.

After learning what had transpired in the apartment and receiving instructions for the circle ritual and smudging, I discovered the young woman following my directions to the letter. She did not even heed my greeting as she carefully circumnavigated the structure. The couple appreciated that the difficulties were resolved as promptly as they had arisen.

My decades-long experience with clearings came in handy when my late husband, who had a horrible temper, visited his mother in a nursing home.

I decided to perform a covert clearance because he was rude to me for no reason. When he went, I rushed about the home with the doors and windows open, smearing everything to hell. As I prayed, I could feel layers upon layers of energy lifting.

Following the smudging, a water bottle mister containing oils of eucalyptus, sage, cedar, pine, and peppermint was used. During the clearing, healing music with a high frequency was also played. I then prepared a mixture of a rose quartz stone and peppermint/sage/chamomile tea in the teapot.

The bottle of massage oil with rose, sage, amber, and eucalyptus was next to my husband's favorite chair. The stereo played soothing music when he returned, wild-eyed and looking for a fight.

I invited him to sit down, poured him a cup of aromatic tea, and inquired about his day. As he spoke, I massaged his head, neck, and shoulders with the special oil. Without speaking to him, I prayed for his freedom in silence.

Twenty minutes passed until he sighed, releasing all the bad energy he had stored. Twenty minutes later, his soul was cured. "How did you know?" was his initial question.

The following question was, "How did you do that?" (his mother was a mental vampire; she had drained him of so much energy that he was on the verge of becoming physically ill) Your place can be cleared with such ease and efficiency.

What do you do when you feel trapped in a rut when the energy around you is stagnant, whether at your house, business, car, or even within yourself? There are many possibilities, depending on what energy is sluggish, where it is and why it is so stagnant.

Stagnant energy can be created by different factors, including negative thought patterns, behavioral disorders, closed-off energy sources, an accumulation of energetic imprints or garbage, and a prolonged absence of cleansing issues. To combat these challenges, you have some solutions; thus, remain open to the possibilities that resonate with you.

A basic smudging technique can be used to purify a room on a basic level and is ideal for residential use due to the smoke. Depending on where you get them and your inclination, smudge sticks may include either pure sage or a mixture of sages.

Light the smudge stick and walk round the interior perimeter of the room or entire house, fanning the smoke into corners and around doors and windows to disperse stagnant energy and improve the energy flow throughout the space or house.

You can produce a crystal elixir for smudging to purify an office environment on a broad scale. Create an Amber elixir, let it charge for one hour, then spritz it lightly throughout your workspace. Avoid getting any electronic devices wet in this mist.

For spiritual purification, be careful to use lapis lazuli and clear your aura fields with big clockwise sweeping gestures. You can also utilize a brushing method that moves from above your head chakra to the floor and around your entire body.

For energy grid cleansings, use Ammolite in your dominant hand during the session to break up stagnant energy on all grid levels!

CHAPTER 11
SMUDGING RITUALS FOR PURIFICATION, RELAXATION, AND MEDITATION.

At the beginning of a significant occasion, smudging is a traditional ceremony that can be performed solo or in groups. As we pause to analyze our physical, mental, or emotional health, the practice of smudging can become a highly useful method of "checking in."

Smudging can be used to raise awareness of what is occurring. It can also act as a potent instrument for restoring our equilibrium and re-rooting us in our bodies and a better energetic-emotional state.

It employs traditional methods and simple instruments, like herbs, plants, and our intuition and/or sense of smell. Traditional societies hold the belief that smoke attracts negative energy. As the smoke dissipates, it brings the negative energy with it and releases it in a location where it can be changed to positive energy, such as composting.

The sense of smell produces strong emotions and recollections. The nose delivers information to the brain more directly than any other sense. This functions as a safety warning, alerting us to an imminent threat. Even our metaphors demonstrate the subtle yet intense nature of our sense of smell: something smells fishy. Something smells bad. We detect the odor of a rat.

The sense of smell imparts taste or flavor to many foods. If you completely plug your nose, it becomes difficult to discern between an apple and an onion. Quite awesome!

We naturally prefer pleasant and sweet odors. This reassures the deepest parts of the brain that the world is safe. Because of this, firms go to great lengths (and trust me, they do) to ensure that their products smell a certain way. However, this can also confuse the brain, as it is "educated" that everything is "happy" and secure when this may not be the case.

Before the invention of chemical odorants, many cultures employed essential oils, perfumes, and plants to fragrance the air. In the Middle Ages, evergreen boughs were used to "deck the halls" during the holiday season. It was a technique to bring in fresh air during the winter when all windows were closed, and people disliked bathing. Yuck!

Smudging is a method for purifying the air and returning sweetness to our lives, both physically and figuratively. This usage of smoke and incense is referred to as "smudging." This is still practiced by churches, especially during significant or unique services.

As he enters the church, the priest carries an incense container, which he waves before him. The fragrant smoke wafts in front of him and throughout the congregation. This works to purify the air, expel negativity and calm the soul.

This is referred to as "making sacred space" or "opening sacred space" in indigenous parlance. This ritual of burning incense or smudging establishes a boundary. Previously, we were ordinary; now, we have gathered for a specific reason.

This is a reminder to set aside external thoughts and concerns, such as disagreement with a partner or spouse, car maintenance, and job-related problems, as they are all irrelevant to what is occurring internally. Instead, we are in the current moment.

In older cultures, many objects served this function, and the choice of attire often depended on the occasion. In the same way, plants have distinct physical and therapeutic capabilities. They also have distinct magical and ceremonial applications.

Traditionally, smudge sticks are tightly-wrapped, string-bound bundles of dried plants and herbs. This facilitates simpler handling and a steady, gradual burn. Native North Americans often employ sage, sweet grass, and cedar. Each culture utilizes what is native to its environment. This is essential.

While it is occasionally beneficial to bring something from afar and to value what is not locally available, it is essential that we work with and forge connections with the things in our environs and owing to this fantastic resource known as the Internet, identifying plants and comprehending their functions is as simple as clicking a button.

I reside in New England and am familiar with some available, practical, useful plants. For broad applications, mugwort, cedar, and herbs are excellent. They serve as the foundational elements.

They can be utilized as-is for general use and support. They can also be combined with other plants and herbs to increase their potency and specificity. It is similar to cooking. However, the goal is to make something unseen but felt rather than something visible and edible.

Now we have a little understanding of what a smudge stick is and the practice of smudging. However, what is smudging? How do we do it? What is its purpose? And how does it work?

You can use anything that produces smoke or incense to smudge. Occasionally, you can understand why you are smudged. Perhaps you experienced a difficult day, a disagreement with a buddy, a love split, job loss, or death.

Sometimes we cannot pinpoint the source of a problem. Something has a fishy odor. This may be an appropriate time to smudge. We can also smudge to commemorate or protect a positive thing, such as a new job, romance, or birth.

On the energetic-emotional level, Smudge functions as light or insecticide. Things that do not belong will flee or be eliminated/killed. Smoke from smudge is comparable to placing a towel over an invisible person.

We cannot see the invisible man but perceive his form and movement through the cloth, and when we are energetically depleted, it feels as though our nose is plugged. We cannot always distinguish between apples and onions. Smudging cleanses the bubble's energy field, and we can distinguish what must be eliminated from our bubbles and lives.

Smudging is comparable to meditating. It can be comparable to dusting furniture. There may be a specific event occurring. We may be aware of what is happening and learn to detect where it is hiding within our bubbles (the energy field around our bodies) or perform a smudging ritual to spend time in our bubbles, investigate it and clear away things as we encounter them.

Also, it is possible and advised to smudge spaces. Negative energy is eliminated from a room or building via smudging. The act of smearing can alleviate tension in a room following an altercation.

Smudging can eliminate traces of previous occupants when moving into a new home or apartment. Like painting the walls, smudging imbues the room with your unique energetic, and emotional imprint.

Okay, so how do you accomplish this?

Start the show. Set aside some time for alone. This is similar to meditation; you should be in the current moment. Especially at first, you are still learning how to smudge and what techniques work best for you. Take your smudge stick and hold it for a time in silence. Do you know what you are seeking and attempting to release? This time is comparable to developing an action plan.

What do you wish to achieve? Perhaps you feel something is holding you down and wish to clear it away or provide clarity to something elusive. You should concentrate even if you do not know or have a clear objective. As you gain experience, this becomes less difficult than it initially seems.

After completing this, light your smudge stick. Inhale deeply into the smudge stick. In practical terms, this enables the smudge stick to produce smoke by creating a solid ember. You are energetically and emotionally blowing your intention into the smudge stick.

It resembles quantum entanglement, while the smudge stick represents the bloodhound. You are providing it with the aroma it seeks. Then you must have faith in its ability to seek or find its prey.

Gently move the incense stick within your energy bubble. Your bubble stretches approximately an arm's length in all directions: circular, like a bubble, front, back, sides, and bottom. You could already have a notion of where something is lurking in your bubble.

You can need to proceed carefully through your bubble. Using both hands is beneficial. One holds the smudge stick while the other investigates the bubble immediately preceding the smoke.

This work is comparable to a blind person reading Braille: a light and delicate touch is required to perceive what the eyes cannot see. Is there a spot where your fingertips somewhat catch? Is your hand speeding up?

Possibly a region will feel somewhat warmer or cooler. Have faith in your intuition and utilize intuitive imagination. As memories make their way to the surface, you can have recalls. You can envision rocky, sticky, or even empty terrains.

Utilize the smudge stick and smoke to purify the space when you discover places where anything might be hiding. Like window cleaner on glass or a mirror, wipe and dab the dense area. Explore the entirety of the space within your bubble. Explore close to your body and the outskirts.

Spend additional time on the three energy centers: the forehead representing wisdom and thought. The heart represents emotions, and the abdomen represents actions and physical aspects. Tend to every area and facet as the situation dictates.

Consider it your patient or your child. Most things and people desire to belong, to feel secure, cherished, and protected. What does it require to be whole, happy, and energetically moving?

Fill this void with love, compassion, and illumination. This will repair your bubble and your soul. The healing will assist you in moving forward in life and achieving more tranquility.

CHAPTER 12
SPIRITUAL HOUSE CLEANING WITH SAGE SMUDGING.

You can have heard the phrase "spiritual housecleaning" and wondered what it meant. As if normal housekeeping weren't sufficient, right? A spiritual spring cleaning can be useful. American Indians adopted this as a means of eliminating undesirable 'negativeness.' They utilized incense and herbs for spiritual house cleanings and to encourage favorable effects in their dwellings.

Sage was a prominent herb used by American Indians. This is known as "Smudging." The dried leaves are typically packed and tied to make a sort of sage "wand" or pole. These were then lit and burned as incense, and the smoke was transported throughout the living space.

The smoke from the sage is utilized to remove unwanted influences from the area. Following this, they often employ the herb Sweetgrass to promote favorable impacts. Often, these were accompanied by prayers, blessings, and mental images.

The American Indians and nature-based and peaceful religions, such as Paganism and Wicca, continue to use this practice extensively. They believe that, like individuals, a place's energy can be disrupted by negativity. For instance, the negative impact remains if something bad occurs in a home. The same holds for positive things. They utilize equipment to "purify" the home of negativity.

This is the typical procedure for 'cleaning' a home. Commonly employed herbs include Sage, Agrimony, Angelica, Basil, Sweetgrass, Frankincense, and Myrrh. Typically, the person will have to carry the burning herbs (in a heat-resistant censer) through each room of the home while 'visualizing' any harmful energy leaving or being cleansed by the smoke from the herbs.

Typically, this is accompanied by prayers requesting their God to remove any negative. They will move throughout the entire house, repeating the visualizations or prayers in each room.

People of all religions engage in this "spiritual housecleaning" because the rewards are substantial. People claim that their homes are safer and 'feel lighter' You can also accomplish this by sprinkling the herbs about the windows and doors and anywhere you suspect there may be negativity.

The law of attraction states that anything you picture will become a reality. Thus, some individuals assume that imagining alone will be sufficient. This is a widely held notion; even celebrities, professional athletes, and millionaires claim to utilize visualization and energy herbs to achieve their goals.

If you decide to execute a spiritual housecleaning and wish to employ herbs, please conduct a thorough study, as some herbs can be poisonous, particularly when burned in the home.

Spiritual Housecleaning is a good and beneficial thing; if only these plants could do the dishes!

House and house cleanings can be performed for different reasons. I am referring to an energetic spring cleaning to eliminate negative and stagnant energy, energetic debris, ground energy lines that can cause damage, electromagnetic wave interference from spiritual entities, and household appliances that feed off energy spots. It sounds like a lot and might be difficult, but I will describe a few straightforward methods for cleaning your home on your own.

Using a smudge stick made with sage is a simple and effective approach to eliminate negative energy and stagnant air. Light the end of the smudge stick, then carefully and gently extinguish the flame until the stick is burning through the sage and producing copious amounts of smoke. Sage can be mixed with other herbs, but most of the mixture should be either sage or a sage-based mixture.

Circulate the interior perimeter of your home while blowing smoke into all corners and around all windows and doors. Using a white feather enables this procedure to blow smoke into such nooks with animal spirit's purity.

Marcasite may also be utilized for crystal smudge. Before smudging your home, use this crystal's vibrational frequency to charge a smudge stick. If you want to use crystal smudging solely, you can charge a bottle of purified water with Marcasite for 24 hours and mist all areas of your home, ensuring you get into corners above and below and entryways.

Tibetan singing bowls can be used for home purification with sound vibrational frequency. Each bowl has its unique vibrational frequency and is based on the needs of the home and the intention behind the vibrations; the correct bowl should be used for this particular session.

Place rock salt in the corners of each room after a cleansing session to help integrate the energy work that was accomplished, use incense, place wind chimes throughout the home, light candles and have flowing water foundations, among many others, to help cleanse and clear an area.

All these things maintain an energetic flow throughout your home, preventing the accumulation of energetic garbage. Remember to clean your home at least once every month to maintain its cleanliness and flow.

CHAPTER 13
ELIMINATING NEGATIVITY IN THE NEW YEAR FOR YOU.

Being in the company of negative people might alter your disposition and ruin your day. Our day occasionally forces us to confront the challenge of interacting with family members, coworkers, and others who fill the air around us with their misery, fear, hatred, and jealousy. This causes us to be submerged in bad emotions.

As a clairaudient and clairsentient psychic, I receive calls every day from individuals who have been dragged through circumstances rife with negativity and seek advice on how to neutralize or eradicate the destructive effects of negative energy. To comprehend what you are experiencing or facing, you must distinguish its appearance and sensation.

Negative energy manifests as nausea, disorientation, and exhaustion. You experience heaviness in your chest or shoulders. Some get migraine-like headaches, while others experience an increase in anxiety, as it is natural to "flee" a negative environment.

Then, how does positive energy feel? Positive energy feels like enjoyment and delight, a giggly mood. It is essential to realize that negativity clings to those who anticipate it or participate in it. Although it can be so aggressive that it clings to you, your business, or your house, there are ways to decrease its impact on you and your surroundings.

Epsom Salts should be your primary form of defense. Soak in a tub of warm water to which double the amount of Epsom salts have been added. Soak your entire body, including your hair.

Once the water has cooled, shower and shampoo with your usual cleansing agent, then dry yourself and don clean clothing. Immediate hydration is necessary, as the bath will leave you dehydrated. If possible, take a rest; a nap is better. To improve the cleansing properties of your bath, try burning white sage at home.

Even smudging yourself before or after a dip with Epsom salts is permissible. To accomplish this, ignite the bundle of sage and pass it over the exterior of your body, starting at the soles of your feet and moving upward over your entire body.

I also recommend that clients increase the cleansing environment of a bath by lighting white candles, burning sage, and playing music to generate a meditative state for emotional relaxation. Smudging with sage or cedar is another effective method for dispelling unpleasant, depressive energies. You can smear yourself, your home, your office, and your vehicle.

Smudge sticks are available at metaphysical bookstores, health food stores, and gift shops. To produce the necessary smoke for smudging, ignite the end and extinguish the flame. Pass it between your armpits and legs and let the smoke rise on your clothing.

When your energy is low because you've spent time with negative people, you should also pass sage over yourself slowly and breathe in deeply and calmly. You will immediately notice the difference.

Keeping key parts of your home or business tidy is essential for warding off negativity. Negativity will conceal itself in chaos, filth, grime, and cobwebs. After a day packed with negativity, burn a single leaf of sage in a safe container to ensure a tranquil night's sleep.

Throw away outdated newspapers and magazines and return them to their respective cabinets and closets. Vacuum, dust, mop, and wipe until all surfaces feel clean. Using a pleasant lemon aroma or Pine-Sol cleanser will also improve your mood.

Lightly spray a pleasant room deodorizer throughout the home and if it is a sunny day, try to open the doors and windows for at least fifteen minutes. Once the space has been thoroughly cleaned, use smudging to dispel any energy that you believe to be negative.

In Feng Shui, it is recommended to position a mirror immediately opposite the entryway to deflect negative energy before it enters the home. Observing what occurs when a negative individual enters an energetically pure environment is fascinating.

They object and simply refuse to enter. Another space purification approach is peeling one orange and placing the peels in a water bowl. Spend more time where the energy appears denser as you walk through your home and flick the water about it.

When a space has been neutralized, all that remains is to fill it with pleasant thoughts, prayers, or natural products - especially flowers. You will know the cleansing was successful when the area seems lighter, safer, and more comfortable.

Walks in the fresh air, deep cleansing breaths, exercise, yoga and meditation, and surrounding ourselves in white light - especially when performed regularly - can all send negative energy back to its natural place in the cosmos and make us less susceptible to it.

CONCLUSION.

Smudging is the practice of cleaning your home with smoke from a bundle of sage or cedar. Smudging is the act of smoking or smudging your living area with a smoldering bundle of sage or cedar. This cleans the rooms in two ways: first, by catching airborne pathogens, and second, by removing the room's stagnant energy.

I have conducted smudging many times without incident. It has always proceeded as smoothly as possible. Walking around with a broom and clearing the air of airborne diseases and other spiritual detritus was as routine as dusting.

Getting a nice smoke from the sage is typically the most difficult aspect of smudging; I must use many matches or an empty butane lighter to keep the sage blazing. So this time was going to be different. I had a two-inch diameter sage/cedar smudge. I separated the twigs to allow oxygen to get deeply into the bundle.

I had to restart it two or three times, producing the desired amount of smoke. I would blow on it to keep the embers going and finished. I reside in a modest flat. I am always exceedingly cautious with fallen embers so as not to ignite my apartment.

I placed the sage in an old pie tin on the table and sat to enjoy my freshly smeared apartment. I believed I must have done an amazing job because I could smell sage. I began reading my book without much thought, but after an hour, my small dog began acting strangely, and I felt a burning sensation in my throat.

Occasionally, the sage may burn itself out in the pie pan, and I then rinse it under water. This time I was successful, although previously, I had failed because I was able to get the sage to burn like never before. This time, the bundle had been burning, it's grey/white smoke twisting and curling and filling my apartment with its distinct odor.

It wasn't a particularly warm day, but I opened the window and turned on the fan. I donned a fleece sweatshirt and socks to stay warm and began to consider which was worse: a cold apartment or a smoke-filled flat.

I attempted to maintain a delicate equilibrium between being chilly and avoiding smoke inhalation and frostbite. Do I maintain the heat with all windows open? This appeared to be counterproductive.

My dog has a thin coat, so I wrapped him in a blanket, and we both braved the cold. He glared at me accusingly; yeah, I knew I had caused this hardship. The smudging was a gift that continued to give.

After three days of balancing daily airings and staying warm, I believed the smoke had been eliminated, but my sister complained about the odor a few days later. She has an abnormally sensitive nose, so once again, cool, fresh air saves the day.

I am uncertain if this was the intended outcome; do you smudge to eliminate diseases and harmful psychic energies? Alternatively, is getting rid of the smudged odor truly cleaning?

It's like when they add the scent to natural gas because it's odorless in its original state; it's a warning system, so smudging is like getting rid of things that don't have a smell; nevertheless, when you get rid of the smudging smell, you know you've gotten rid of everything else as well. Next time, I will practice better fire safety procedures, wait for a warmer day so I can leave the windows open, and perhaps the dog will stop giving me evil looks.

This book is part of an ongoing collection called "Using Sage and Smudging"

1. Learning About Sage and Smudging
2. Sage and Smudging for Love
3. Sage and Smudging for Health and Healing
4. Sage and Smudging for Wealth and Abundance
5. Sage and Smudging for Spiritual Cleansing
6. Sage and Smudging for Negativity.

Other Series by Sherry Lee

"Learning About Crystals"

1. Crystals for Love
2. Crystals for Health
3. Crystals for Wealth
4. Crystals for Spiritual Cleansing
5. Crystals for Removing Negativity.

Why Alternative Medicine Works

1. Why Yoga Works
2. Why Chakra Works
3. Why Massage Therapy Works
4. Why Reflexology Works

5. Why Acupuncture Works
6. Why Reiki Works
7. Why Meditation Works
8. Why Hypnosis Works
9. Why Colon Cleansing Works
10. Why NLP (Neuro Linguistic Programming) Works
11. Why Energy Healing Works
12. Why Foot Detoxing Works
13. Why Singing Bowls Works.

"What Every Newlywed Should Know and Discuss Before Marriage."

1. Newlywed Communication on Money
2. Newlywed Communication on In-laws
3. Newlywed Communication about Children.
4. Newlywed Communication on Religion.
5. Newlywed Communication on Friends.
6. Newlywed Communication on Retirement.
7. Newlywed Communication on Sex.
8. Newlywed Communication on Boundaries.
9. Newlywed Communication on Roles and Responsibilities.

"Health is Wealth."

1. Health is Wealth

2. Positivity is Wealth
3. Emotions is Wealth.
4. Social Health is Wealth.
5. Happiness is Wealth.
6. Fitness is Wealth.
7. Meditating is Wealth.
8. Communication is Wealth.
9. Mental Health is Wealth.
10. Gratitude is Wealth.

"Personal Development Collection."

1. Manifesting for Beginners
2. Crystals for Beginners
3. How to Manifest More Money into your Life.
4. How to work from home more effectively.
5. How to Accomplish more in Less Time.
6. How to End Procrastination.
7. Learning to Praise and acknowledge your Accomplishments.
8. How to Become your Own Driving Force.
9. Creating a Confident Persona.
10. How to Meditate.
11. How to Set Affirmations.
12. How to Set and Achieve your Goals.
13. Achieving Your Fitness Goals.
14. Achieving Your Weight Loss Goals.
15. How to Create an Effective Vision Board.

Other Books By Sherry Lee:

- Repeating Angel Numbers.
- Most Popular Archangels.

Author Bio

Sherry Lee. Sherry enjoys reading personal development books, so she decided to write about something she is passionate about. More books will come in this collection, so follow her on Amazon for more books.

Thank you for your purchase of this book.

I honestly do appreciate it and appreciate you, my excellent customer.

God Bless You.

Sherry Lee.

Made in United States
Troutdale, OR
07/18/2023

11363116R10062